Fire

from

Above

René Kieda

Fire from Above

by:
René Kieda

Published by:

The Riehle Foundation
P.O. Box 7
Milford, OH 45150 USA
513-576-0032

Published by The Riehle Foundation
For additional copies, write:

The Riehle Foundation
P.O. Box 7
Milford, OH 45150-0007 USA
513-576-0032

Scripture quotations used by permission of:
Good News for Modern Man © 1966 American Bible Society,
© 1967 Broadman Press Nashville, Tennessee and the *New
American Bible* with revised New Testament © 1986
Confraternity of Christian Doctrine Washington, D.C.

Cover illustration by: Christian Wilhelmy

Library of Congress Catalog Card No.: 97-065720
ISBN: 1-877678-46-5

To my Mother, Mary

THE DUNGEON

My feet dangled out the open door of the helicopter taking me on my last ride over the Vietnam jungle. *Home...home...home,* the rotor blades above my head seemed to say. But a voice inside me competed for my attention.

"What are you going home to, René?" the voice asked. "What's the purpose of your life? For that matter, what's the meaning of anyone's existence?"

I had no answers. I didn't know who I was, why I was alive, or what I was facing when I returned to the states.

"Jump!" the voice in my head screamed. "Jump... jump...jump...."

Blood seeped into my mouth as I ground my teeth into my cheek. But even pain couldn't stop that voice urging me to throw myself from the helicopter into the void of self-destruction.

How do you escape from your own head?

How do you find relief when the horror sits inside you? Where do you find hope and a place of rest when your life choices have propelled you into a pit of darkness?

My darkness began before I could make a choice. It was in Rome, Italy, 1948. My mother conceived me out of wedlock and we became the talk of the neighborhood. Later, she became pregnant with my sister and quickly married an American professor and magazine writer who was visiting Rome.

Unfortunately for me, Mom dabbled in the occult and was marked for life by a fortune teller who told her she was going to die a horrible death. She became obsessed with the thought. In fact, one of my earliest memories is of her telling me she was going to die.

"No, Mommy," I cried. "You're not going to die. I won't let you!"

But she insisted and from early childhood the fear of her death and my impending loss was constantly with me.

When I was four or five, we traveled to America by boat and settled in the lower east side of Manhattan in a neighborhood of Italian, Jewish, and Hispanic families. My stepfather was a broken man who found solace in liquor.

He lived a life without purpose, aimlessly wandering from job to job with no goals or direction. When drunk, he would lash out at fate and sometimes at those close to him. There was no faith, no prayer, no belief in our home. Only a constant wailing about the futility of life.

When I turned seven, we moved to sunny California, but I was still surrounded by gloom. Pop could never find the right job, and my mother complained constantly about our living conditions. We moved five times during those five years. My memories are mostly of loneliness and a life in limbo—no direction, no purpose, no meaning.

Finally, my parents decided to return to New York where they rented a one–and–a–half room apartment in a basement on 22nd Street and 8th Avenue. I called it *the dungeon.*

The sun never seemed to shine in New York. The tall buildings shadowed the dirty streets and set the tone of my teen years. It was 1961 and the beginning of the Hippie cultural revolution. Our neighborhood was a haven for prostitutes, homosexuals and drug addicts. I wandered the streets taking the darkness into my soul.

Love might have made a difference in those formative years. But love was nowhere to be found. Pop was either totally withdrawn or drunk. He and my mother had been verbally abusing each other for years as I sat on the sidelines filled with rage at my inability to stop them.

Then one day, when I was eleven-and-a-half, I spoke up for her. It felt good to be finally old enough to shout with the others. But when words progressed into a fight, I was out of my element. Five feet, three inches, one hundred pounds is no match for a five foot, nine inch, two hundred and fifty pound drunk.

Pop slapped me around a little while I lashed out and miraculously managed to get in a few hits. Mom stepped between us; but, as he tried to reach around her to get to me, he slipped and hit his face on the bed post. I was petrified when this hulk of flabby flesh shrieked with pain and cursed the air. With his attention diverted, I ducked into the closet and slammed the door, holding onto the handle for dear life. Mom wailed, he bellowed, and I shook so hard the door rattled. My poor sister cowered in the farthest corner.

"You're not my son," he screamed at the closed closet door. "You're nothing but a little bastard!"

The words sliced through my heart like a hot spear. How could that be? I called this man, Pop. He was my Dad. As pitifully inadequate as he was, beneath all his drunken abuse, I always felt he must love me, at least a little. After all, I was his son. But I no longer had that assurance. I couldn't call him Pop, and I hated him for that. Hated him with a passion I had never experienced.

Mom didn't explain why she had lied to me all those years. "He" never apologized; and I never brought the subject up. Maybe I should have. But I didn't; instead I internalized the rage, hate, and rejection and lashed out in confused disrespect. The darkness that began before my birth was complete. Love no longer existed. No more pretenses, no more lies. The relationship with both parents was over and, for all practical purposes, the person I had been was dead without a proper burial.

THE HOOD

The street became my home. I attended seventh through ninth grades at P.S. 3 on Hudson and Christopher Streets in an Italian and Hispanic neighborhood in Greenwich Village. After school each day I would go home to eat, but as soon as "he" came in I would leave. I wouldn't return until I knew he had collapsed into bed in a drunken stupor. Many times it was in the early hours of the morning before I would let myself in.

My mother tried to talk to me, but there was nothing she could say that would heal my wounded spirit. I vacillated between hate and pity for the both of them. I suppose I should have tried to help my sister, but by now she was a total shell of a girl who quietly endured it all. I, on the other hand, was fighting to survive.

And survive I did! Over the next few years, I began to do dope and drink. Then I joined a street gang. The Undertakers had an initiation ritual I had to pass. In order to become a member, I had to walk the gauntlet. Two rows of guys lined up across from each other—about twenty on each side, some of them muscle-bound weight lifters. As I walked between the rows, each of the guys punched and kicked me shoving me back and forth between them until I finally made it to the end of the human tunnel. I wanted to scream from the pain, but I made it to the end without opening my mouth. The test wouldn't have been too bad, if that had been all. But it wasn't. The hard part was that I had to turn right around and go back through again until I made it back to the point from which I had started. Taking that first step back was tough. This time, I knew what to expect and I wasn't sure I'd get through without falling down or crying out in pain. Fortunately, I made it. I was black-and-blue for weeks, but at least I didn't end up with broken bones like some of the others.

The gang became my substitute family; they made me feel important. I belonged there, they cared about me, and best of all I finally had a reason and purpose for my life. Of course, the purpose wasn't anything to be proud of. Drugs, alcohol, theft—I did it all. I was even shot at twice by the police.

I was fifteen on the night of the infamous Northeast blackout. I had hooked up with some of the Undertakers in Washington Heights looking for excitement on an otherwise boring evening. We ended up in a grocery store grabbing goodies and stuffing them inside our baggy jackets. Then we separated to leave the store and joined up later at our favorite hangout, a small tunnel by the subway entrance. We spent a lot of time there scouting out the girls as they went by on their way home from school.

This night, when the electricity throughout the Northeast went out, the only light came from a full moon. Cars snarled at intersections, horns honked, people yelled, and we laughed at the mass confusion. Drunk from the beer and wine we had lifted at the store, we added to the clamor on our corner. In fact, we were downright rude. So, before we knew it, a bunch of cops were lining us up against the wall, waving their nightsticks in the air and threatening us with them.

When one of the Undertakers dropped a beer bottle, the cops mistakenly thought he intended to use a broken bottle neck as a weapon. A nightstick pounded across the back of the guy next to me; another slashed the legs of the kid on the other side. But I wasn't touched.

"Get the wagon!" one cop yelled. Then he radioed for reinforcements to lock us all up and that was all I needed to hear.

No way I'm going to prison, I thought as I pushed my nose against the brick wall. We were now all lined up against that wall with our arms in the air, just waiting for the paddy wagon to come to take us away. I was pretty proud of the fact that I was one of the fastest runners in my high school, so I decided to make a dash for it! The cops were standing about five feet away when I crouched down and sprinted to the street. It was pitch black and they were caught by such surprise they just couldn't react fast enough to catch me.

A number of police cars with flashing lights were lined up outside the tunnel and some of the guys from the gang were hiding behind them watching. As I dashed out of the dark, I ran smack into an old man. I screamed at him and shoved him out of my way as I sprinted down the street with several of the cops after me.

"Stop or I'll blow your head off!" one bellowed.

The moon was ahead of me and I kept my eyes on it as the adrenaline poured through my body and into my legs. Every nerve strained toward freedom.

No way I'm stopping, I thought, *you're just going to have to blow me away!*

Time was suspended; eternity loomed. The moonlight beckoned as I waited for the bullet to pierce my brain. No sound. No impact. NO BULLET!

Around the corner, down the dark streets, into the night I ran. My heart raced, my lungs burned, but I made it. I was free!

Joey and Tony met up with me a little later that night. "Hey, Kieda Man!" they said. "The cops are looking for you. The one that tried to shoot you aimed but then he tripped on the curb and fell. He broke his hand. You're some lucky dude, Man."

Many of the gang had been arrested, and we worried they would rat on us. But after a few days, they were released and none of the rest of us were brought in for questioning.

When I got my license I bought a used red Chevy convertible with a white rag top. I was some popular dude as my buddies and I cruised the streets with the top down. One summer day, six of us decided to drive downtown to scout out the Greenwich Village area. As we stopped at a street light on Canal Street, a souped up roadster pulled up next to us. The driver revved his engine. I revved mine back at him. When the light changed, we took off with tires burning rubber. We raced down two city streets neck and neck with police sirens blaring behind us. When I realized that the light at the next intersection had just turned red and the traffic was crossing our path, I slammed on the brakes and the Chevy went into a screeching slide that lasted for the entire city block. The girl that was with us screamed for the whole time and her baby wailed along with her. The car stopped a mere ten feet from disaster.

The squad car pulled up behind me and two cops jumped out. When one of them reached my door, he started shouting. After he finished his lecture and gave me a warning, he let us go. I remember his parting words: "You're either a damn good driver or somebody up there likes you."

I should have learned my lesson from that close call, but of course I didn't. I drove the Chevy into the ground and then bought an old MG sports car. It was a real status symbol at the time. One Friday night, Jose invited me to a gig (party). We hopped into the MG and headed toward the apartment on 16th Street and 9th Avenue. Jose had some prime stuff with him, so we were smoking pretty good as I drove. I held my breath so long that suddenly I blacked out while we were driving down one of the side streets. When I came to, I realized we were heading straight into the back of a parked trailer truck and I couldn't do a thing about it. We hit and the windshield caved in and came to rest an inch from my face. Glass and metal surrounded me, but when I got out of the car I didn't have a scratch on me. Jose, on the other hand, had cuts all over his face. We made our way to the hospital and then took the subway home. The MG ended up in the junkyard. Once again, I was miraculously spared.

When I was 16 I met a girl at a neighborhood youth dance. I was immediately attracted to her, so I asked her for a date. She told me she would like to go out with me, but her parents wouldn't let her date anyone who wasn't of the same religion. She suggested I change my name to Richard Cohen and then we could go out. I was too stupid to realize why I needed to change my identity, but I thought *why not, it's only for a few dates*.

The relationship lasted for more than three years and I was Richard Cohen for the entire time. It was especially difficult at family gatherings when people would call *Richard* and I wouldn't respond immediately. It was even worse when I didn't have a clue as to how to participate in some of the family's traditions. I just pretended to be a religious dropout. Once again, I was without a true identity.

First love—how exciting that is! Sarah satisfied part of my need to feel wanted and to have someone who cared about me. At times, my feelings for her began to fill the emptiness that had been in my heart for as long as I could remember. But the void was never completely filled.

We became sexually active and I was obsessed with the relationship. The sex became addictive, but at times I felt suffocated by the relationship and wished I had never gotten involved. It was weird to love her one moment and hate her the next. The emotional turmoil was, at times, too much to bear.

Several times, Sarah thought she might be pregnant and she panicked. To me, the whole thing could be dealt with as a nuisance. I looked for ways to abort this glitch in our relationship with no thought at all to an unborn child created in our image. Fortunately, each time Sarah was wrong and we celebrated. Of course, we never learned our lesson and we continued to flirt with danger. But the pregnancy scares and Sarah's emotional demands forced me to look at the responsibilities of the relationship and I became more depressed than ever. I tried to break things off several times, but each time my intense desires and the emotional bond that physical intimacy creates pulled me back to her. Then fate intervened.

It was 1968—the Tet offensive in Vietnam, the height of the sex and drug revolution, the British rock bands, the anti-war demonstrations and the assassination of Martin Luther King, Jr. The streets were getting hotter and tension increased as I sank deeper into gang life. It wasn't a time for anyone to be hanging out on the streets.

One day I tried to talk to my mother about life. "Why am I alive?" I finally asked.

She looked at me with deep sorrow.

I begged her for an answer, but she didn't have one. She was as helpless and as desperate as I was.

Depression—that feeling of having a bottomless pit in my gut—was my constant companion. Waves of hopelessness would swallow me up if I didn't keep moving. The futility of life had become so burdensome that I wished I had never existed.

I thought about suicide, but was afraid to botch the job. What I really wanted was to have not existed at all, ever. Life didn't make sense to me. Mom had made it clear when I was very young that there was no afterlife, nothing to look forward to but death. So, I thought, if there's no afterlife and each person exists for only a short time, why try to succeed at anything only to lose it when you die? That concept became deeply rooted in my teenage heart.

Miraculously, I made it all the way through to graduation from Aviation High School, a trade school in Queens. Then I went to work on Wall Street installing and repairing phone systems for New York Telephone. That job might have catapulted me out of the hole I was in, but in May I received a letter from the government. I was drafted and was I thrilled.

"Finally, I'm getting the hell out of here," I told my friends.

I didn't realize the Vietnam war was at its height. I was just relieved to be getting out of the war in which I was living. Any place else had to be better!

DRAFTED

The draft I was called up in, in 1968, was President Johnson's big build-up. More than 500,000 troops were going to be stationed in Vietnam. So, when I arrived at Fort Jackson in South Carolina for basic training, the base was a hotbed of activity. Soldiers running, screaming, moving by the thousands.

Since there was no room for us new recruits in the barracks, they assigned us to makeshift tents. There was no doubt most of us were on our way to Vietnam. The feelings of excitement and urgency of purpose surrounded us like a thick cloud.

I suppose I should have been scared. But, I wasn't. I didn't support or oppose the war. I didn't have an opinion about much of anything. From the time I was sworn in by the Army recruiter, René Kieda no longer existed. I was merely a number in a sea of humanity. I was nineteen and lost; caught in a world I couldn't control.

The second day in camp I was stripped of all my possessions. My head was shaved and I was issued baggy fatigues. The next morning we recruits were shocked out of a deep sleep before sunrise. The men gathered for roll call on the blacktop in front of the tents. As the sun began to rise and the rays of light illuminated my surroundings, a terrible feeling of isolation came over me. I had finally found the non-existence I had been praying for.

The majority of the troops I went through basic training with were assigned duty in Germany. I, on the other hand, was selected to go to Non-commissioned Officer School at Fort Benning, Georgia.

"This is an honor," my Captain told me. "I recommended you because I think you'll make a good NCO. Don't disappoint me."

My flash of pride quickly fizzled when I arrived at Fort Benning and found some incompetent bureaucrat had admitted me to NCO school without the proper security clearance. I expected them to clear me so I could stay, but they said it would take up to a year to do that since I had been born in another country. So, since they didn't know what to do with me until the clearance came through, they decided not to bother. I was transferred to a holding company at Fort Benning where I waited for papers that would send me to the infantry in Vietnam. I was more than disappointed, I was enraged. The NCO assignment had kept me from getting the training I needed for combat duty; suddenly that training was what I needed the most. Life, once again, was unfair.

But then through what I know today was God's Providence, I was assigned to the K9 Scout Dog Unit where I met Apache, a three-year-old German Shepherd. I had always wanted a dog. Now I had one. I needed unconditional love, and now I had that too. God was filling my needs and I didn't even know He cared about me.

The dog was great, but the job we were assigned to was a killer. Apache and I were trained to walk the point. That means we would lead the infantry units through the jungle, swamps, and trails of Vietnam. With Apache's keen sense of hearing and smell, he was supposed to detect ambushes, snipers, and booby traps, such as trip wires, before I walked into them. If the scent was fresh and the wind blowing our way, Great! Otherwise, it was mere chance that the dog would give me an early warning.

Apache became my best friend. It was sad to think that if we made it out alive, I would be sent home, but Apache would stay for the duration of the war. We remained at Fort Benning for nine months as we underwent training. Then, just before we were to join eight other soldiers and their German Shepherds on a military transport heading for the war zone, I was given a three-week pass to go home. I looked forward to getting back to the old neighborhood and planned on some heavy partying with my friends after touching base with my parents and Sarah.

But once I got home, my excitement quickly turned sour. I felt like I was in No-Man's Land. My life had changed drastically and I suddenly realized that even though I was only twenty years old, I might never see these people again—ever! I visited some of my friends and went to a few parties, but the more I tried to enjoy myself the worse I seemed to feel. It was as if I had a terminal illness and the doctors had only given me one month to live. At times, waves of grief and panic would overwhelm me.

Since I felt like I was seeing Sarah for the last time, I decided I should make some gesture that would cement the relationship and make the last three years we had spent together mean something. I asked her to marry me. I don't know if I felt I owed that to her or to myself. Sarah was thrilled. She truly loved me and promised to be faithful to me while I was gone.

The three weeks raced by and before I knew it I was standing at La Guardia Airport saying good-bye. My mother, sister, and Sarah cried as I kissed and hugged them. Pop looked old and beaten to me as we shook hands. I walked away and never looked back.

Apache and I were soon on the transport heading for Bien Hoa (ben wah), where we would be on call for use by different infantry platoons in the area. Our job would be to lead patrols through the Vietnam jungles. Tension was high during the eighteen-hour journey. This trip was a one-way ticket to hell and we all knew it. The noise from the jet engines made it almost impossible to talk without shouting. But then, none of us felt like talking. We were numb! Reality was rushing in and we all suddenly realized we might never see our families again. In fact, one day soon, we might never be seeing anything again.

As the trip droned on and the dogs settled down, I thought back to a morning during training when an old sergeant had instructed 200 of us recruits on the dangers of ambush.

"Expect that 90 percent of you are going to die in an ambush," he shouted.

He got my attention that day and held it as he outlined types of ambushes we should look for—L-shaped, U-shaped, I-shaped. Here was a man who had served in WW II, Korea, and now Vietnam and he was standing before us, alive. His making it through to tell the story stayed with me then and helped me on this day as Apache and I roared toward our fate. *I guess if the Sergeant can make it through three wars, I can make it through a year*, I thought.

Then we descended into Saigon's Ton Sun Nut airport and I walked into the stifling 100 degree plus temperature; any positive thoughts evaporated in the heat and stench. The humidity made your skin feel as if you hadn't washed in weeks. Your body felt like it was caked with oil. Dust and dirt swirled everywhere as helicopters, jets, and prop planes took off and landed in a continuous stream of urgency and excitement. As far as the eye could see, transport after transport landed, unloaded, and took off again and again and again.

We unloaded our dogs and placed them in the shade in a nearby building. After seeing to Apache's needs and settling him down, I went outside to watch the planes. One cargo plane was of particular interest as skid after skid was loaded, each skid holding a dozen aluminum boxes. My curiosity got the best of me and so I stopped a guy who was walking by and asked him what was in them.

"They's all dead bodies, stoopid!" he answered. "Welcome to the Nam."

IN COUNTRY

Apache and I were assigned to the 59th Scout Dog Platoon located in Duc Pho, south of Chu Lai. The platoon consisted of eighteen dog handlers who went out in rotation. When intelligence reports of enemy activity came in, a company or reconnaissance unit would request a scout dog team to accompany them on their mission. Each of the missions consisted of three to five days of scouting, then a day back in Duc Pho to rest the dogs, then back out on another mission with another platoon.

The night we arrived at the main camp, we were welcomed by an incoming mortar attack. That sure got this city boy's attention! My life was on the line as the camp was pounded by the heavy shells. The dogs barked, dirt flew, and men ran for the bunkers—another shocking reminder of where I was.

27

In less than a week, I was busted for drug possession. At first I was scared. But then I thought, *What can they do to me? I'm risking my life in this hell hole for a year and for what?* No one had explained what I was there for. No one had talked about a cause we were fighting for. They trained us to do a job and then told us, "Obey orders and stay alive."

Of course, there was mention of the Communists but no real explanation of what that meant in this situation. Since I had been brought up with so many diverse nationalities, the word "commie" was just another term for people as far as I was concerned. We weren't encouraged to debate moral principles, all we had to know was how to identify the enemy, and that seemed easy.

They were the little guys dressed in black pajamas wearing straw hats. They were the sneaky guys that couldn't be trusted. Ever! They were the guys who planted mines and attacked you when you were at your weakest, then disappeared. They sounded like the Assassins, a street gang I knew in New York.

The weird thing was that this enemy could be a local peasant who pretended to be friendly, but who was really Viet Cong (VC). He would kill you if you let your guard down.

Even women and children couldn't be trusted—also like the old neighborhood.

The goal of this war was to stay alive. Each of us was on our own. It was our only reason to fight. Nothing else mattered. You fought to survive one more day. Exactly the existence I had just come from but much more intense.

After my drug bust, in May of '69, I was assigned to the American Division, 11th Infantry Brigade, 59th Scout Dog Platoon, Duc Pho, South Vietnam. I was no longer a good boy so I couldn't be sent to exceptional divisions like the 101st Airborn (Screaming Eagles) or the First Division (Big Red One). I had become fodder for the largest and one of the worst disciplined divisions in Vietnam. Because this division suffered so many killed and wounded, the soldiers nicknamed it the "Casualty Division".

I soon found out that the brigade I was assigned to—one of the three brigades in this division—was known for some of the worst atrocities in the war. The 11th Infantry Brigade was home to a company whose men disobeyed a direct order in war time. It also was the brigade known for the massacre at My Lai, and several more such incidents. Here I was, at their mercy. One more grunt (foot soldier) being sacrificed on the altar of national pride.

Duc Pho was a beautiful area near the South China Sea, and yet it was forbidden to us because it was full of VC. But then, in reality, nothing is beautiful when you're in a camp in enemy territory and surrounded by barbed wire.

Drugs and alcohol flowed freely. There were few people who weren't using something to escape the fear and boredom. Of course, I was doping and drinking with the best of them. Just like in the old neighborhood.

Then I met Freddie, a junkie from Brooklyn who introduced some of us deeper into the world of hard core drugs. The night I made that leap, five of us were huddled in a sandbag bunker on the perimeter of Duc Pho. Freddie was twenty-two, but he looked thirty-five. Medium height, stooped at the shoulders, with an air of constant, twitching nervousness about him, Freddie's eyes gleamed as he prepared to induct a few more lost souls into his private hell.

The five of us bragged about our drug experiences as an odd sense of anticipation and excitement settled over the filthy bunker. Dust swirled around our heads with each gust of wind. Conditions were far from sanitary when Freddie pulled out the long plastic tube that would be wound around my arm to restrict blood flow so my bulging vein could invite the dirty needle into my body. Then spoon and matches were pulled from Freddie's bag—and finally, pure opium.

This small black ball of dope was placed into the spoon, the match lit and held under the spoon. As the opium began to melt and bubble, soot from the match settled on the liquid along with the dust falling from the sandbagged roof above us. Then Freddie placed the needle into the center of the spoon and began to draw the oozing liquid into the syringe.

When it was my turn, the vein in my arm popped out in welcome and with a sly wink and a smile, Freddie injected me. The liquid felt warm as it entered my bloodstream.

I waited for the high, but instead I got sick...really sick. Excruciating pain slammed into my joints and stomach. My head felt as if it would burst wide open. My whole body ached as if it had just been beaten to a pulp by an angry gorilla. I spent the longest night of my life curled into a fetal position in the dirt wishing, hoping, and praying the pain would go away or that I would die. It was almost more than I could bear, but I couldn't cry out for help. Medics would have reported me, and my buddies were all in a stupor. Each of us was trapped in our own private hell. A hell we chose to enter.

TRIAL BY FIRE

That experience didn't help my nerves any during my first mission. In fact, the mission was an emotional disaster. I was teamed with another dog handler and we made quite a pair. He had about thirty days left to go before he could climb aboard "The Freedom Bird" for home. Most of his time was spent counting the days, trying to stay alive, so scared he barely spoke. I, on the other hand, was as green as the rubber trees in the jungle.

When it was time to go, we loaded supplies on a helicopter until there was barely enough room for me and Apache. I sat on the deck of the chopper dangling my legs in mid air. Apache settled in next to me. I held onto him with one hand and grasped the support bar with the other as we lifted off from the ground and headed toward our destiny. My heart tried to jump out of my chest when the chopper rose above the trees and leveled off at a few thousand feet.

Below us, the valley blended into different shades of green under the blazing sun. I had a tough time keeping Apache in the chopper because he kept trying to stick his body as far out as he could so he could feel the cool air. After we both settled down, I could have flown around up there all day. But, unfortunately, we had a mission and it was about to begin.

As the chopper sank toward the landing zone, the jungle mesh enveloped us. I noticed a trail of smoke and realized it came from a helicopter that had been hit by sniper fire and had crashed at our destination point. I didn't have to be told to watch myself.

We landed in a clearing about twenty-five meters from the nearest platoon and hit the dirt running. Then we made our way under cover toward the troops gathered near the burning machine.

That's funny, I thought, *why are they dressed in white?* As I got closer I was amazed. The white I thought was cloth was really caked-on sweat that had dried into the men's fatigues. It looked like splotches of white paint. My clean, green fatigues stood out as clearly as if I were wearing a sign: *Fresh meat approaching.*

A Captain took us aside and showed us a map. "The NVA (North Vietnamese Army) are in the area," he growled. "Our job is to find them and draw them out."

What he didn't say was that it wouldn't be easy. It was certainly no surprise we were here. The enemy had already shot down one chopper and killed several men. There was no doubt they were waiting for us. We were at a disadvantage because we didn't have a clue as to how many men we were up against. In this northern section of South Vietnam it could be a considerable number of NVA troops. We, on the other hand, had only about ninety men in the company, evenly divided into four platoons.

The Captain wanted one of the dog teams to lead the company through the jungle giving advance warning of the enemy or finding any booby traps the NVA had placed along our path. The other team would trail behind one of the platoons and be used as backup. It was no surprise to me that the other dog handler, my new "buddy," graciously volunteered Apache and me to lead the way. We were to "walk the point."

The men lined up behind me ready to move

out. I was assigned a rifleman and a grenadier to walk behind me. If I didn't get blown apart by a booby trap, or have my brains blown out by a sniper, they were there to give me a little support if we stumbled into enemy troops.

I placed the harness on Apache so he would go into search mode and we started out. "Find 'em, Apache. Find 'em, boy," I urged.

The seasoned troops were no calmer than I was. The tension had a presence all its own. As I led the group through heavy vegetation and along some trails to our first destination, I was so cautious it took us all morning to travel the length of about two football fields.

Since the enemy often carried livestock for food, I froze when I heard a rooster just out of sight. A clearing lay at the bottom of the hill and the Captain decided to gather the troops at a point there and wait for further orders.

By now the men were sweat covered, tired, and emotionally drained. We had started out in the early morning; it was noon when Apache and I finally broke out into the clearing.

How did I ever get myself into this? I thought as the sweat poured out of me. Apache sniffed the air in the direction of the bushes in front of us and the hair on the back of my neck tried to pull itself out by the roots. I quickly checked behind me for my backup, but found emptiness. The troops were hiding in the bush and I was the sacrificial lamb waiting in the open for someone to blow my brains out.

I crouched down and made my way back to the tree line so I could report what seemed like enemy activity up ahead. Not one of the waiting men looked me in the eye as I passed by.

After I reported the crowing rooster and Apache's nervousness, the other dog handler told me we were going back to the base.

"But, we just got here," I said. "We can't go back until our mission is completed."

"I don't give a damn," he said. "We're going up that hill over there and getting out on the next supply chopper."

Since the Captain had decided to resupply the troops before going any further, some of the men were busy clearing a landing zone (LZ) at the top of the hill.

The senior dog handler ordered me to follow him to the LZ. He was so afraid we would miss the chopper and have to spend the night in the jungle that he kept yelling at me to hurry up. The more he cursed at me, the madder I got. I was furious. The pack on my back weighed more than seventy pounds. It carried equipment, ammunition, and a three-day ration of food and water for me and Apache.

The hill was straight up and it became harder to climb with each step. But no matter how hard I strained, the bastard in front of me kept screaming curses at me. I didn't care if he was responsible for bringing me back with him; all I wanted to do was unload twenty rounds into his back.

And I could have done it easily! Each time Apache's leash tangled in the underbrush, I came closer to murder. But, instead, I beat the poor dog. If he hadn't been a willing scape-goat, I would probably be in prison today serving a life sentence for murder because of the volcanic rage I could barely control.

Halfway up the hill, I threw my helmet away. I couldn't manage the dog on one hand, the M16 in the other, and the helmet rocking around on my head. Besides, there was no reason to put up with that irritation anyway. Sure, the helmet might save my life; but my life wasn't worth saving, so why bother wearing it.

When we finally reached the top of the hill, one of the grunts handed me a hot beer. I thanked him and gulped the liquid down just as if it were the coolest drink in the world. Another one of the troops had found my helmet and carried it up the hill even though he already had over ninety pounds on his own back. He handed it to me without a word as he went by. These two acts of kindness quenched the rage that boiled inside me.

We finally got back to base. The "idiot" was one mission closer to going home alive. I, on the other hand, made certain I would never be assigned to patrol with him again. "Throw me in the brig or do whatever you have to do," I told the Lieutenant, "but I'm not going out with that asshole again. Ever!" And, I didn't. I never wore my helmet again either.

The days passed by: mission, after mission, after mission. Apache and I at point, our lives hanging in the balance. We would spend three or four days with different companies in the brigade. I never knew what to expect, nor did I ever feel like I was part of the troops. No one cared about me. I was always the outsider—totally expendable.

On one search and destroy mission near the My Lai area, we landed in the late afternoon on a high mountain overlooking a beautiful valley with many villages. We were to join other infantry units coming from the north and south in the valley at dawn. Our mission was to move all of the villagers to refugee camps. We were also ordered to destroy the houses, livestock, and food supplies.

The Captain called me over as soon as Apache and I landed. He described the mission and told me that we needed to get to the bottom of the mountain by dawn. That meant that I would be leading the troops down an unfamiliar mountain path while it was pitch dark with the possibility of enemy snipers and booby traps ever present.

As we began to start down the mountain at dusk, I saw two Vietnamese men running for cover in the valley. They immediately aroused my suspicions because from sunset to sunrise all villagers were forbidden to move freely about the land. The entire area had been designated a free fire zone. Anyone found out and about from this time in the evening to early in the morning could expect to be shot at.

The Captain decided the men I had seen were setting up an ambush so he called in an artillery strike from a nearby U.S. firebase. Unfortunately, the strike overshot the target and the 155 millimeter Howitzer shells exploded on our position. Shrapnel flew everywhere as the men cursed. We could hear the Captain screaming into the radio, telling the firebase gunners to stop. Larry, one of the dog handlers, was hysterical. "We're gonna die! We're gonna die!" he screamed over and over again. He was driving us crazy. A few of the guys tried to go over to him to force him to shut his mouth, but Larry's dog, King, wouldn't let them near his master. His growling and barking added to the confusion surrounding us.

I grabbed Apache and held him close as we hugged the dirt and hoped for the best. In the sudden silence when the barrage finally stopped, I heard the guy lying near me whisper, "Thank you, God."

Being hit by friendly fire was not the way to start a mission with confidence. Everyone's nerves were now on supercharger as the darkness fell and the command came to move out. I could barely see Apache in front of me as we made our way down the mountain. I could hear men stumbling and falling behind me. Their curses rang out in the still night air and the equipment clanged and rattled. If enemy troops had been in the immediate area, they could have targeted us for a strike just from the noise and confusion.

We finally reached our assigned quadrant just before sunup. We regrouped and then headed into the first village.

We found only old men, women, and children left there. Throughout the hamlets, the young, healthy men had been forced or recruited into the North Vietnamese Army. This valley's villagers had been given notice a few weeks before that they should proceed to the nearest refugee camp, but many had refused to leave their homes and birthplaces. I felt sorry for them. They were caught between the United States' forces and the NVA. A real no-win situation.

As we traveled through each village in the area, we burned the straw huts, destroyed the food supply, and scattered or killed the livestock so the enemy would be deprived of food and support. Screams of fear and hatred from the women and children pierced the air when our torches ignited the homes of these country people. As I looked out across the valley, I could locate each village by the cloud of acrid smoke rising from it. The dark smoke erased the skyline and blotted out the sun.

Fortunately for my sanity, there were a few times when humor broke the stress for a moment.

As we were searching and evacuating one village, Apache decided to chase a few chickens. He was on a twenty-five foot leash at the time so that if he tripped a mine (booby trap) I would have at least a small chance of survival. When he started to chase the chickens, the leash wrapped around me. Somehow it pressed on my trigger finger and my M16 fired. At least seven rounds went off as guys around me dove for cover. I looked more than stupid as I sheepishly stood there with my arms pinned to my sides and my dog circling closer and closer. Thank God, no one was hit.

Another time I was leading an infantry unit on patrol to flush out reported NVA regulars in the area. As Apache and I pushed through some dense vegetation, I decided to take an easier route through a dry river bed. Unfortunately, the bed went up a steep incline. I was struggling up this hill when one of the grenades attached to my shoulder straps came loose and bounced down the bank behind me. It was really quite funny to see each of the guys behind me diving headfirst into the surrounding brush to escape the runaway grenade.

Such light moments out in the bush were few—in fact those are the only two I can remember. The rest of the time that year I felt like someone was pointing a gun to my head playing Russian Roulette with me. I never knew when a booby trap, a sniper's bullet, or an ambush would sign my death warrant. The trails we walked looked innocent enough, but one wrong move often meant a quick trip to oblivion. You would think that the more I got used to the routine, the easier it would get. But the opposite was true. Each mission brought greater tension. The pressure mounted as the odds of survival grew slimmer. How many missions would it take before my luck ran out? When would the bullet with my name on it finally get to the firing pin?

I had to laugh when I remembered our training sessions. We were told that if you made it through the first three months, you were well on your way to a safe tour. They should have told that to the guy behind me who had two weeks left in the bush and got his head blown off.

THE FIRST CALL

By September, my nerves were raw. Apache was keeping me alive with his radar-like nose, but the summer offensive, the heat, and the increasing reports of American men being murdered and mutilated had worn me down.

One morning, I was standing by my bed in our canvas tent enjoying a slight breeze blowing in from the South China Sea. We had no mission planned and I looked forward to the day of rest.

Suddenly, a voice called my name. *"René!"*

I didn't even look around. There was a warm feeling around my chest and a sense of well-being. I knew the penetrating voice came from deep within me. It was kind, gentle, personal, fully accepting and totally loving. Yet it had an urgency to it. There was no talk of my sordid past or any accusations of wrong doing. Just my name breathed in unconditional love.

I don't know how, but I recognized the voice. The name that came to mind was Jesus and I responded to that inner voice with a heartfelt cry of recognition.

"Jesus," I whispered and a surge of joy flowed through me. It filled the emptiness and displaced the loneliness that had been part of my life for as long as I could remember.

"Follow me!" the voice instructed.

Although this experience lasted for only a few brief seconds, it was enough to change my life forever. Love called and a new creation was born.

I walked out of the barracks and looked at a sky dotted with puffy white clouds. Then I climbed on top of the bomb shelter and languished there in the bright sunshine. Never in my unhappy life had I felt like I did at this moment—totally loved, accepted and cared for.

After about fifteen minutes of savoring the new sensations a disturbing thought entered my mind.

You've got to let her go.

I knew it was a command from Jesus, but it was almost too much to bear. Sarah was one of the few people who had ever shown love for me. Now that I was in Vietnam and feeling so out of sync with the real world, her love and our plans to marry gave me something solid to cling to. She was my link to reality.

"No, Lord, no," I cried. "She's all I have; the only person who truly cares for me. Please don't ask me to give her up."

But the thought didn't go away. No matter how much I resisted, it remained. The message was persistent and gentle and it often made me cry, but throughout the struggle, somehow my spirit knew I would obey.

That evening I wrote a letter to Sarah telling her I was breaking our engagement and leaving her for Jesus.

She'll think I've gone nuts, I thought as I mailed the letter. In the three years we dated, I had never gone to church, never mentioned God, and, other than cursing, had never said Jesus' name in her presence. She would surely think my time in Vietnam had sent me over the edge. But I knew deep inside that the request from the Lord was right for me, so I obeyed.

I'm sure some people will attribute this experience to heavy drug use. Others will say it was due to stress. And I might agree with them if that had been the end of it. But it wasn't! My life was changed in that instant, and everything since then has borne out the reality of the intercession.

I see now that God had to act in a powerful way at that moment in order to save my life. Otherwise, today, there would be no life to write about. I was on the fast track to eternal destruction.

Even though God changed my life in that instant, the war droned on: mission, after mission, after mission. Most of the requests for Scout Dog teams came from troops in the northern section of the 11th Infantry Brigade. As my days blended into each other, the Voice became a memory. My only thought was *stay alive*.

Then one day, between missions, I received two letters. Sarah wrote of her deep hurt and accused me of running away from my responsibilities. Mom's letter told of my stepfather's heart attack and my unmarried sister's pregnancy.

"This is what I get for following you, Jesus," I called out in anguish. "I don't believe in you!"

I totally rejected the Lord and depression hit with a vengeance. I was barely able to drag myself to one more mission before I got so weak and ran such a high temperature, I had to report to the clinic. "You've got malaria," the medic told me. "You're on your way to Chu Lai."

I was transported to Chu Lai Hospital on September 20, 1969, my twenty–first birthday. *What a fantastic present this is,* I thought as I flew away from the battle zone to safety. If I'd known what I was facing, I wouldn't have been quite as happy.

For the five months in-country, I had skipped most of my malaria pills. It was just too much of a bother, and I really didn't care if I got the disease or not. Nothing seemed important enough in my life at that moment to care about it one way or another. I find it interesting that I didn't contract malaria until after I renounced Christ. The timing sure got my attention!

When I settled into the clean sheets on the hospital bed they felt like a bit of heaven; but they soon became overbearing as their very touch increased my agony. My temperature soared to 105 degrees before dropping; then, just as quickly, it would rise again. I felt like I would explode one minute then freeze to death the next. Chills ravaged my body until my teeth chattered. This cycle of oven to freezer, freezer to oven repeated itself over and over until I thought it would never stop.

Along with the malaria, it was discovered that I had a case of gonorrhea. Then, as if this wasn't enough suffering for one guy, one of the medics gave me a shot of antibiotic in the wrong place and partially paralyzed me so I couldn't walk for a while.

But, four weeks later, I was a new man. The recreational drugs in my system had been purged by the fever and I languished in the clean surroundings. No snipers, no booby traps, no dirt or bugs in the food. My only complaint was boredom. The experiences of the past were forgotten. The pain and suffering had wiped out all thoughts of my family, the break up with Sarah, and my experience with Jesus. It was like I was a man without a past.

One day I decided to pass the time by reading *Good News for Modern Man,* a book I picked off the wardroom bookshelf. *This looks interesting*, I thought. *Is there good news for modern man?*

I opened the book and flipped through the pages. Jesus—that name again! The name I had called out in the tent.

Let's see what this man has to say for himself, I thought.

I went back to bed and made myself comfortable. The sun was shining as I opened to Matthew, one of the Gospels. In the narrative, Jesus is speaking to a crowd gathered around him. He is using a parable (a story) to explain the kingdom of God. In this illustration he says:

> *The Kingdom of heaven is like a man who sowed good seed in his field. One night, when everyone was asleep, an enemy came and sowed weeds among the wheat, and went away. When the plants grew and the heads of grain began to form, then the weeds showed up.*
>
> *The man's servants came to him and said, 'Sir, it was good seed you sowed in your field; where did the weeds come from?'*
>
> *'It was some enemy who did this,' he answered.*
>
> *'Do you want us to go and pull up the weeds?' they asked him.*
>
> *'No,' he answered, 'because as you gather the weeds you*

*might pull up some of the wheat
along with them. Let the wheat
and the weeds both grow together
until harvest, and then I will tell
the harvest workers: Pull up the
weeds first and tie them in
bundles to throw in the fire; then
gather in the wheat and put it in
my barn'* (*Matt.* 13:24-30).

Later, in *Matthew*, Jesus explains the
parable:

*The man who sowed the
good seed is the Son of Man; the
field is the world; the good seed
is the people who belong to the
Kingdom; the weeds are the
people who belong to the Evil
One; and the enemy who sowed
the weeds is the Devil himself.
The harvest is the end of the
age, and the harvest workers are
angels. Just as the weeds are
gathered up and burned in the
fire, so it will be at the end of
the age: the Son of Man will
send out his angels and they will*

gather up out of his Kingdom all who cause people to sin, and all other evildoers, and throw them into the fiery furnace, where they will cry and gnash their teeth. Then God's people will shine like the sun in their Father's Kingdom (*Matt.* 13:36-43).

Wow, I thought. *There really is something beyond this life. This isn't the only existence.*

As I continued to read, I realized that not only was there a reason for existence and a future after this life, but I also found that my life was important too.

"*The Kingdom of heaven is like a buyer looking for fine pearls,*" Jesus said. "*When he finds one that is unusually fine, he goes and sells everything he has, and buys the pearl*" (*Matt.* 13:45-46).

Then, in *Luke* 17:20-21, I found the final piece to the puzzle:

"*The Kingdom of God does not come in such a way as to be seen,*" Jesus told the Pharisees. "*No one will say, 'Look, here it is!' or, 'There it is!' because the Kingdom of God is within you.*"

At that instant, my chest cavity exploded with light. *I found it.* I thought. *I found the answer to life.* It seemed like my entire being had opened up and there lay the Kingdom of God within me. I was a fine pearl, not a rotten bum. God had looked into my heart and found me. The real René Kieda. And I knew without doubt that Jesus felt that way about everyone. I had finally found the purpose I had been searching for.

"This is it!" I exclaimed to the guy in the bed next to me. "The answer to life is here in this book."

He looked at me like I had just arrived from Jupiter. I suppose he thought I was still hallucinating from drugs or fever. But he was wrong. For the first time in years, I was clean. My mind was clear; my spirit open. And God had shown me His Kingdom. It was here, in each of us, if we would only open ourselves up to it.

I jumped out of bed and traveled through the ward telling everyone of my vision. "I've found the key," I yelled. "Jesus is the answer to all of life's needs and wants. He is the Way, the Truth and the Life!" (*John* 14:6).

Some of the men cursed, some yelled at me to get away, some just stared in frozen silence, but I didn't care. I knew that after all my years of searching—through the drugs, and sex, and gangs—the darkness had just been lifted and I had been shown the Truth.

Jesus came to establish His Kingdom. This kingdom is in each person. The Lord invites each of us to meet Him there. His love is so great that He doesn't want to wait until we're dead and buried in order for us to join Him in the relationship that forms this kingdom. The shocking, glorious truth is that God dwells within us.

"My Father and I will come and make our home within you," Jesus tells us in *John* 14:23.

We are the temples of the living God. That was our original purpose in the Garden of Eden. We were created to have fellowship with God and to be His holy temple. We do have meaning and purpose. Life is worth living after all.

Within a week I was back in the bush and going on patrol with Apache again. All seemed the same on the outside—dangerous missions, harassment by the officers, drugs and alcohol— but on the inside things were different.

When I got together with my friends I began to tell them about Jesus and the Good

News. They responded, "Yeah, that's great. Let's get stoned." I let it go, but each time we met to get high, I brought the inner kingdom into the conversation. It got so that even my best friends would get up and leave when I started. It was so bad that when a buddy would see me coming, he'd turn and walk the other way.

On my first mission back from Chu Lai Hospital, I prayed the Lord wouldn't let anyone be killed. I knew if I were placed in the position of having to defend myself, I would shoot. There was no doubt in my mind at all. I would act by instinct and training. Previously I wouldn't have given a second thought to the victim, but now the possibility of killing someone threatened my new-found peace.

"God," I prayed, "please keep me from having to take someone's life today." My spiritual experience had brought my conscience back from the dead. God had begun to shape and form me into the man He knew I could be.

In the next few months, the Lord led me into truth about myself. I had many weaknesses and failings. Each day I gave in to one or more of the temptations constantly around me. Each night I pleaded for the Lord to be patient with me.

One day, as I sat on my bed, He gave me a choice. The thought He impressed on my mind was clear. I could either do good or evil. Whatever choice I made at this moment, I knew it would have eternal consequences. I was free to make this choice without coercion or persuasion. It was "rubber meeting the road" time.

I knew I was weak and unworthy, but at that moment I made a conscious choice to do good. And with that choice, it seemed my eyes were opened. I suddenly realized the source of my sin was a deep-rooted selfishness. I had been living solely for myself; no thought for anyone or anything else. This self-centeredness produced sinful acts. As I faced these sins and confessed them to the Lord, I felt like a burden was being lifted off me one layer at a time. I was on a path toward freedom and peace.

The last months of my tour in Vietnam ground to completion and I was finally in the helicopter on my way from the base at Duc Pho to Chu Lai when the spiritual enemy came at me with all his fury.

"Jump, you no good loser!" he told me. "This Jesus crap is a big con. You're still the same, good-for-nothing druggie with no future. Drop out the door, you loser. Life has no meaning. You have no future. Get it over with now. Take the easy way out."

The sweat poured off me as I grasped onto the bar and held on for my life. I tried to pray, but the voice in my head screamed louder and louder with the rotor blades accenting the beat.

"Jump...jump...jump....

Whump...whump...whump."

"Please, God, help me," I begged. Then, in desperation, I shut my eyes tight and held onto the bar beside me until the chopper finally touched ground and I was on my way home.

"Thank you, Lord."

BACK IN THE HOOD

One minute in Vietnam, the next in my old neighborhood. I had lived a lifetime, but had only been gone for a year. Things were different—the streets were dirtier, the guys were older, my parents were grayer—but things were also the same. My friends were still grown-up kids spaced out on drugs and alcohol. My family was still my family. The only thing that had changed was me.

How can this be, I thought as I strolled through the streets. *Don't these people realize men are dying for them? Doesn't anyone care?*

I desperately needed someone to talk to about my two experiences with Christ so I could understand fully what had happened. But, there was no one, so I continued to talk to my friends about Jesus while I popped pills and did dope.

I had been home for about a month when

Sarah called and asked to see me. "Just for old time's sake," she urged. I was certain that my commitment to the Lord and a life of celibacy was the right choice for me. I certainly wasn't looking for re-establishing a relationship based on sex. So when she asked to meet me, I didn't jump at the idea. But since I felt I owed her a face–to–face explanation, I finally agreed to meet her for coffee.

When I opened the door to the coffee shop, my stomach was in knots. Her voice had stirred up memories of our times together that I thought I had buried for good. The bond Sarah and I had established through sex was much stronger than I thought. She looked really good—a little older, but quite attractive. We talked over two cups of steaming coffee, and then she invited me to an apartment she shared with two friends. *Why not,* I thought. *It's fun talking over old times.* So we went, I had some wine, we talked and of course I fell into the trap of seduction.

When I finally left her apartment that day, I was consumed with guilt. What I considered an offense against God came close to destroying me. "How could I have betrayed the One who loved me so?" In agony, I knelt at the side of my bed that night and begged His forgiveness. Then I asked for His help in controlling myself in the future. I don't know how Sarah felt about our encounter, but she never called me again and I didn't call her. It was finally over and my life could go on.

It was time to find some type of job to support my habits. I knew I couldn't face being cooped up in a 9 to 5 workplace, so I decided to work part time driving a cab on the second shift in Manhattan. You meet the best and the worst in New York from 4:00 p.m. to 2:00 a.m.—drunks, prostitutes, partying businessmen— I understood them all.

Although my life looked like it was on track, deep inside I knew it wasn't. You can't reconcile reading the Bible and drug highs with a clear conscience. The Lord Jesus had been patient with me; but, for how much longer? I kept making promises I knew I was too weak to keep. Deep down I loved the dope more than I loved Jesus. But I kept praying and asking Him to be patient with me—again, and again, and again. Unfortunately, my will was still set against this source of Love. I still preferred myself over Him.

One night as I prepared to go out the thought came.

*René, it's Me or the drugs. You **must** decide!*

Time was running out. I knew I had just been faced with one of those decisions in this life that would impact on not only my future but also on eternity. I was pulled apart, torn in opposite directions. The Lord had freed me from my enslavement to sex and I didn't need the gang friendships as much, but I couldn't seem to allow Him to free me from the desire for amphetamines, speed, and marijuana.

One hot, muggy night in August, I overdosed. The Undertakers had been in Fort Tryon Park in upper Manhattan and we had an assortment of drugs to choose from. I tried most. By the time I made it home, I was in serious trouble. My heart raced out of control one minute, then slowed to a crawl the next. I started to heave, and I felt like I was going to pass out and die right there on my filthy bed.

This is finally it, I thought. *I didn't die like a hero, I'm dying like a dog.*

"God, please have mercy on me," I begged. "Don't let me die here, not now. I want to live, Lord. Please deliver me. Please."

The night dragged by as my soul fought with my body. When the rays of day shone through my soot-streaked window, I knew I had made it. I would live. But how would I live? That was my choice.

"God," I prayed, "at the end of the month I'll quit my job and follow you. I know I can't do this alone, so I'll find a church with some people who believe like I do. With their fellowship and strength, I think I can live a Christian life and break away from this sinful life I'm leading. I'm not sure I can, Lord, but I promise to try."

PROMISES TO KEEP

A few days later, I was back at it again. I remembered the promise I had made, and fully intended to keep it. *I can handle it*, I told myself. *At the end of the month, I'll do it.*

But, when the last week of August arrived, I thought, *I'll need some cash for awhile. I'll drive a cab until the end of September, then I'll find a church and turn myself in to God.*

But God had another plan. I came down with an ear infection that kept me from driving. The doctor gave me medication and after a few days rest, I decided to go back to work.

At 5:00 p.m. a couple hailed a cab from in front of Macy's Department Store at the corner of 34th Street and 7th Avenue. I screeched to a stop in joyful anticipation of a quick fare. Greedy for the dollar, I was trying to see how many trips I could make in an hour. Each new fare meant another tip.

"The Bronx," the man said.

"The Bronx at rush hour!" I yelled. "No way." It was the worst time to go across midtown Manhattan to another borough. I knew I shouldn't refuse to go, but greed was stronger than good sense. I would make more with less driving if I stuck to short trips in the immediate area.

"You're gonna take me!" the man insisted.

I had been thinking about going, but when he began to curse me, my pride jumped in and I decided he wasn't going anywhere.

"Take down my hack license number and report me," I yelled. "But get the hell out of my cab. I ain't takin' you nowhere."

In the streets of New York, you learn how to be aggressive. In the jungles of Vietnam, you learn to protect your back. Those were the laws of my world, and I was still very much a son of that world.

I pulled the cab to the side of the street, left the engine running, and got out. I felt cornered and either had to fight or escape. If I fought the man in the back seat, I was afraid I wouldn't be able to control myself and I might do something I would regret for the rest of my life. I feared for myself as well as for him.

The man jumped out of the cab and started screaming curses at me.

"If you're so hot to get to the Bronx," I yelled," take the cab and drive there yourself."

When the lady opened her door and got out, I saw my chance to get away. As soon as her feet hit the pavement, I jumped behind the wheel, revved the engine, slammed my door shut, and yanked the lever into drive. But what I didn't realize was that as I had been doing all this, the man had pushed the woman back into the cab. She had one foot inside and one on the pavement when I took off. So, as I pulled out into traffic, she was being dragged along. Her screams and the cries of the pedestrians finally registered in my brain just as she fell out and the back door slammed shut.

Looking through the rear view mirror, I saw the woman sprawled out on the street on her stomach. The people on the street looked at the scene with horror on their faces. I didn't know if the woman was dead or alive. *"My God, what did I do to Jesus."* The thought struck me right in my heart, but there was no way I was going to stop because the man was a raging fool chasing me on foot down the middle of a street packed with honking rush hour traffic. I knew I couldn't stop or go back. The man was almost insane with rage. And to make matters worse, a gypsy cab (cab without a New York city hacker's license) with two guys in it was also on my tail. They had seen the accident and decided to "get me." They were chasing me down the street like vigilantes with horn blaring and lights flashing just itching to get their hands on me. I knew I was in real trouble now so I frantically looked for a way out of the maze of automobiles. If I hit one car there would be a serious chain-reaction crash, but I didn't care. I just floored the accelerator and hoped for the best.

I raced down the street in the left-hand lane. A construction barricade loomed before me. The middle and right lanes were jammed with cars, but I had to get to the furthest lane on the right to get out of this mess. So, with one foot on the gas and the other on the brake, I swung and inched the cab lane by lane, inch by inch to the far right side. It was truly "a miracle on 34th street" that I didn't hit anyone.

When I finally made it to one of the side streets, I raced full speed towards 8th Avenue. The cars there were at a standstill because of a stalled car. As I approached the intersection, the gypsy cab was still hot on my trail. The light turned red, but so did my fear. It was in the overload zone.

So, I ran the red light. Through one lane of traffic, then the next, and finally down a side street leaving the vigilante cabbies stuck in the traffic at the light. St. Christopher must have been riding shotgun because I sure didn't get through that mess by myself. I wonder if he ended up in a pool of sweat like I did.

When I finally pulled over and got myself under control, I knew I was in serious trouble. I didn't know how badly hurt the poor woman was or even if she was alive. But I did know that the police would soon have my hack number and it was time for me to report the accident before they came looking for me.

"I'm sorry, God," I prayed. "I know I promised to stop driving and seek a church at the end of August. I'm sorry I didn't. But if you'll just help me one more time, I'll keep my promise to you."

I drove to the nearest police station and turned myself in. The desk sergeant told me I was lucky. The woman hadn't been seriously hurt. But, almost before he got the words out of his mouth, the man who had been chasing me appeared. As soon as he saw me, he was in my face. They separated us and took me off to be booked.

A week later we all appeared downtown, at the Courthouse, to answer the charges for the accident. Since the lady had been hurt, the prosecutor wanted to press additional charges and raise the offense from a misdemeanor to a felony which carried a heavier prison sentence. I was facing a possible three to five year jail sentence for reckless endangerment.

On the way to my booking for the new charges, I ran into an old buddy of mine from the streets. He was a cop now. It was unbelievable to me that out of the more than 50,000 cops in New York City, I would meet one at this moment who was a friend of mine. I felt this was a sign that God was with me and helping me get through this mess I had made.

I told my former friend what was going on. "Oh, I thought you were in here for drugs," he said. "Why don't you file countercharges against the man for harassment." Then he told me how to go about it and I did as he said.

It turned out that they booked us both—mug shots, fingerprints, and all—then threw us into the same holding cell with twenty other men waiting for night court. I felt like Daniel in the lion's den as I prepared myself for a beating. But the Lord protected me once again and I wasn't touched. We finally appeared before the night court judge and the case was held over to a new court date later that year.

There was no doubt now that my time was running out. I couldn't go on much longer on my own before something serious would happen that would affect the rest of my life. It was inevitable. Of course, nothing could be more serious than denying Jesus Christ and His call to live in His Kingdom. I knew if I continued to walk away from Him, I would end up in jail or dead on the streets just as many of my friends had. It was time for me to take a stand for life.

CHOOSE LIFE

Sitting in the jail cell that night waiting for a beating, I realized it had been one year since I had found the answer to life. It was the anniversary of my first vision of the Kingdom, and here I was still on the road to destruction. *Wake up, René,* I told myself. *You can't turn your life around by yourself. Get some help!*

When I left the cell that night, I left as a humbled human being. I gave myself over completely to God and waited to see where He would lead me.

I was like a blind man slowly regaining his sight as I submerged myself in the Bible instead of wandering the streets with my friends. It was hard for me to believe, but suddenly drugs held no appeal for me. I was so into studying the Word that I didn't have time to think about the addiction. My Bible was so marked up with notes and comments, it looked like a personal journal. The desires, the yearning for the high, all the attraction of drugs had all but disappeared. I had been freed, truly freed!

"Lord, please show me the church You want me to be in," I prayed. "I need fellowship with other people who believe in You."

While I had been doing this studying and personal seeking, my stepfather had been watching me. One day, when he was somewhat sober, he tossed a pile of literature about different church denominations on my bed. As I skimmed through the pile, I came across a catechism of the Roman Catholic Church and began to read. To my astonishment, the gospel stories I had been reading matched the catechism I held in my hand. It was as if I were seeing a mirror image of those Gospels. The excitement I felt at that moment let me know the Lord was steering me to that church.

Wow—what a relief! All of the other churches in the neighborhood had truths, but this was the church the Lord was leading me to. My search for like believers was over.

I literally ran to the nearest Catholic church and found the parish priest. "I want to join your church," I exclaimed. He must have thought I was a bit zealous, but he welcomed me and gave me instruction.

As I completed my instruction and prepared to receive my First Communion, I found I would be required to participate in the Sacrament of Confession first. To confess my sins to a man was an extremely difficult thing for me to do. I absolutely dreaded it. *Why can't I just confess to God?*, I thought. But then I remembered the words of Christ to his Apostles:

> *Then he breathed on them and said: Receive the Holy Spirit. If you forgive men's sins, they are forgiven them; if you hold them bound, they are held bound (John 20:22-23) (NAB).*

The day of my confession came. As I waited in the pew for my turn, I was so nervous all I could think of was escape. But I stayed and finally entered the confessional booth. "Forgive me, Father," I began and as I laid out my sins before the Lord and His earthly servant I could actually feel layers of guilt and grime begin to be wiped away. When

I was given my penance and received the priest's absolution, I felt reborn. I couldn't remember the last time I had felt so guilt free and clean.

I made my First Communion at Saint Elizabeth Church in Washington Heights on the corner of Wadsworth Avenue and 187th Street. Later I met an ex-Franciscan monk who worked in the parish. He introduced me to the Legion of Mary and I grabbed on to that lifeline and clung to it for dear life.

The Legion is a lay organization (a group within the Catholic Church) that works like a military unit. Ten to twelve people meet each week to say the rosary, learn a teaching of the church, and perform ministry for others. I was the only one under fifty in my group, but age has no bearing when you're a new creation. Each person is new in Christ every day because we all are going through a life–long process of change. Through the Legion, I found self-discipline, people of like mind, and a purpose in life. Without it I would have floundered and sank back into the darkness that surrounded me.

After a long nine months of dread, the court case finally came to an end. All criminal charges were dropped and the injured couple were pressing civil charges against the taxi company. When the charges against me were dropped, I approached the couple in the hall outside of the courtroom. "Please forgive me for the hurt I've caused you," I asked. "I'm very sorry for all that has happened."

The man and his wife both looked astonished, but they accepted the apology and as we shook hands I knew that God had once again set me free.

My days were full of ministry and study now. I tried to witness to members of my old gang, but they didn't want to hear about it. I had found a better way of life, but they were still bound by drugs, sex, and booze.

One night as I was going to a prayer meeting, I passed an old man on the corner of 184th Street and Broadway. "Hey, Kieda Man, watcha doin'?" he yelled as I hurried by.

I turned and for a moment didn't have a clue as to who was calling my name. Then I recognized him. *No! It can't be,* I thought. *This derelict can't be Mike.* The man I remembered had been a good looking, Irish kid that all the girls had their eyes on. But now standing before me was a haggard person with scars on his face and a mouth accented by missing and blackened teeth. He scared me. This one-time teenager who loved life and looked forward to adventure every day had been reduced to a hopeless heroin junkie.

We talked for a while, remembered some of the good times, and I caught up on the people I had known just a few years before. So little time had passed, but so much life had been lived. As I said good-bye and walked away, Mike called after me. "You know, Man, you're about the only one who's made it outta here."

There but for the Grace of God, go I, passed through my head as it did time and time again when I walked the streets of the old neighborhood.

New Beginnings

Living and seeking the Kingdom of God was more exciting and adventurous than anything I had tried up to that time. The inner spiritual life was like a vast cosmos that kept revealing itself little by little. The surprises and intimacy one feels in the Lord's presence was more than I ever thought possible.

"Eye has not seen, ear has not heard, nor has it so much as dawned on man what God has prepared for those who love him" (*1 Cor.* 2:9) (NAB) .

I was working as a shipper while also doing street ministry with the Legion of Mary. Since my life had changed, I had come to a better understanding of my parents. I recognized their emotional pain and reached out to them with a softer heart. As my life changed, I brought less stress to the home front and there was finally a semblance of peace in the house. Our relationship wasn't perfect, but it got a lot better when money I saved helped the family get out of debt.

Exactly two years after my initial meeting with the Lord, and one year after joining the church, I followed what I thought was a call to the ministry and enrolled at the Holy Apostles Seminary in Cromwell, Connecticut. My future seemed assured. I was on God's track and I was going to be a priest. But the Devil didn't let me go without one last attempt to drag me back into the old life.

Several weeks before I was to enter the seminary, an old army buddy called me. He was depressed and begged me to meet him at a corner bar on the east side of Manhattan so he could talk out his problem. I agreed. My plan was to give him an hour or so before I went on to an all-night prayer session being held at St. Francis of Assisi Church on 33rd Street and 7th Avenue.

We met. He talked. And after a while, he seemed to feel much better. It was a help just to get his feelings out to another person who had experienced the horrors of Vietnam.

We left the bar together and began to walk

down Second Avenue when suddenly I felt someone come up behind me and before I could turn around my eyes were covered by two soft hands. "Guess who," a familiar woman's voice called and I recognized Sarah. When I turned to see her, my breath caught in my throat. She was wearing a skin-tight dress with a plunging neckline. As I introduced her to my army buddy and they exchanged pleasantries my self-control seemed to be oozing right through my body and out my toes. So, when she invited me into the bar to meet her friends I followed like a lamb to the slaughter. She introduced us to everyone; then my buddy left and I was alone with Sarah. After some light conversation, she decided it was time to leave and asked me to accompany her home. We took a taxi to her apartment building, then stood outside talking in a darkened doorway. My control had gone long before and I was trembling with desire. Sarah asked me to resume our relationship and promised me it would be even better than it had been before. The more she talked, the more desperate I became. Finally, I sobbed out in surrender the words, "What do you want me to do!"

The tone of my voice said more than my

words because without another word, Sarah turned and walked into the apartment building and out of my life forever. It was a miracle because if she had stayed or made some move toward me I wouldn't have had the strength to deny the temptation. Later, in the prayer meeting, I thanked God for saving me from myself once again.

The following week I entered the seminary thinking my life was following a Divine plan. But after several months of spiritual struggle, I finally realized that what I had thought was God's call on my life to enter the priesthood was more in my own mind than His perfect will. I struggled greatly as I tried to find what the Lord Jesus had in mind for me.

One day, after Christmas break, a friend from the seminary asked me if I would like to go with him to the hospital to visit Mr. Murphey, an elderly man who was well-liked by the seminarians.

"Sure," I said. "I don't have anything else to do today."

Later, as we stood by Mr. Murphey's bed looking at a picture he had drawn, a nurse walked into the room.

"Hi, Mr. Murphey," she said.

I didn't look up, but when I heard that voice I knew without a doubt this was the woman I was going to marry. I was so certain she was the one the Lord had chosen for me to spend the rest of my life with, I announced the fact to my friend as soon as she left the room.

But, of course, after I got back to my room and really thought about marriage I wasn't quite as certain it was such a good idea. My parents' marriage was a disaster. I couldn't see myself spending a lifetime like that. And it was a ridiculous thought anyway! After all, I knew God had called me to be like St. Francis, a spiritual warrior. I wanted to be a monk and undergo strict discipline and hardship for the Kingdom of God. I had enjoyed the spartan lifestyle I experienced in the Army. Now I could live such an existence in my spiritual life. To me, marriage was a sign of weakness. People who got married instead of devoting their life to Christ in celibacy were weak. They just didn't have what it takes. But after several months of intense prayer and personal sacrifice, I finally realized that the Lord Jesus wanted me to enter into the Sacrament of Marriage with the woman I had met at the hospital. I did a 180 degree reversal in my thinking and set out to follow my Lord's direction.

I went back to the hospital with my friend to see Mr. Murphey, but I was really looking for the nurse. I introduced myself and found out her name was Debra. By the time we left that day, I had asked for a date. Deb agreed if my friend would join us and we would have dinner at the apartment she shared with her two girlfriends.

On our second date I asked her to marry me. "I know without a doubt that this is God's plan," I told her. "He has brought us together and I'm sure you're the one He wants me to spend the rest of my life with." She, of course, thought I was crazy. But after hearing my story and thinking it over, she miraculously believed me that that was God's will for her too. Deb had given herself to Jesus when she was sixteen. She was a member of the Covenant Church in East Hampton, Connecticut and believed deeply in the Lord. Seven months after my proposal, we were married.

Since that marvelous day, we have built a life together. We married before we really knew each other well enough, but every marriage, no matter how perfect or how much in love the two people are, requires a lot of hard work. To live as one with another human for the rest of your life requires strength of character, patient endurance, and a ready willingness to forgive. God has blessed our marriage and has given us five wonderful children.

He also brought healing to my other relationships. I was able to help when Dad suffered a stroke and Mom's health problems made it impossible for them to stay alone in New York. They needed to be closer to family. Deb and I invited them to Connecticut but the Florida sunshine sounded more appealing than the New England cold. I helped them move to Fort Lauderdale and they spent the last three years of their lives together there. My sister and her husband took wonderful care of them. It gave me great comfort to know that both Mom and Dad were reconciled to God and received the last rites of the church before they died.

Working in the kingdom

I have worked in the computer industry for over twenty years. My career has allowed me to provide for my family and I thank God for opening the door to it. I especially thank Him for the ministry He has given me through which I can witness to others about the marvelous changes that happen in a life given totally to the Lord.

In the past ten years, I have actively worked with parish youth ministers recruiting and arranging a way for young people to experience the inner kingdom.

Jesus said, *"But you will receive power when the Holy Spirit comes upon you"* (*Acts* 1:8). Many of our young people have experienced this power. When they do, hope dawns, eternity becomes real, and they begin to have a sense of life's purpose. I have seen this happen at Life in the Spirit Seminars, Youth 2000 retreats, and the High School Summer Conferences at Franciscan University in Steubenville, Ohio.

Somehow, some way, the veil that separates us from the living God drops and these young people experience the soft, gentle stirring heat in their chests that I felt in Vietnam. Most are moved to tears because of the great tenderness they feel reaching out to them as Jesus makes Himself known. It is interesting to note that Luke's Gospel also tells of such a heat when he describes the burning heat the disciples felt when Jesus spoke to them on the road to Emmaus.

"Were not our hearts burning inside us as He talked to us on the road and explained the Scriptures to us" (*Luke* 24:32)(NAB).

During one High School Conference at Steubenville, where 3,000 teens gathered on retreat beneath a massive tent, a fifteen-year-old teenager received a beautiful gift from the Lord. Within herself she could see that Jesus was in each and every person in that tent. Somehow, in some way, she understood that God was in everyone.

In the same tent that weekend, a young man received a vision. He saw himself landing a plane on an aircraft carrier. Today that young man is pursuing the dream and the Lord is confirming the vision.

These teens and others like them have found that God wants good for His people. At one Youth 2000 weekend a young lady heard Jesus' voice calling her to a deeper spiritual life in His kingdom. She came alive at that time!

On the other hand, there are those who come away from such weekend retreats feeling they have received nothing. One fourteen-year-old was quite upset when he told me, "I got nothing from this." Many of his friends had received wonderful graces and gifts, but he had come away empty handed.

"Why do you think you got nothing?" I asked him.

He thought for a moment and then answered, "Because I was afraid!"

"Why are you afraid?" I asked him. His answer surprised me.

"I'm afraid that this God is going to take me over and I'll lose myself," he said.

So many times such fear robs us and keeps us from doing or being what we could do or be. This young man was right, he had missed something at the conference. But he had also received something. He had received the gift of wisdom. When a fourteen-year-old becomes wise enough to understand what is happening within himself, he has gained a powerful gift. It may not be as evident or as spiritually flashy as a vision or an inner voice, but it is most definitely a gift from the Creator who loves and cares for His people.

How many gifts from God have you received and yet you weren't even aware of them? How many times has God acted and protected you in your life, and you don't even know it? If you think back on your life and ask the Lord to show you the times He has intervened, you might find you have been in the palm of His ever-caring hands for a very long time.

As a prison chaplain I meet many young men who have had a spiritual awakening while in prison. They come alive with the realization there is a God and this God is personal. Many repent and serve out their time in holiness trying each day to walk with the Lord Jesus. Regardless of the crime, Jesus Christ comes to them with His love and invites them into the eternal kingdom.

I met one inmate who was about twenty-five years old who had uncontrollable fits of anger. He would lash out at other inmates or at the correctional officers without reason. So, when he was let out of his cell, he was always in chains. Handcuffs circled his wrists and ankles. These restraints were connected to a larger chain that was tied to his waist.

"See those chains on your body," I told him. "They are nothing compared to the chains wrapped around your soul that are keeping you a slave for life." He stared at me and I could see what I had said hadn't really gotten through to him. But I knew he would only too soon realize that the prison cell inside his soul was worse than any cell the correctional system could put him in.

True freedom comes from within, from knowing Jesus Christ. Jesus said the truth will set you free (*John* 8:32). He also said, "*I am the way and the truth and the life*" (*John* 14:6). I pray that this prisoner, as well as others I speak to, will eventually discover the Truth.

Another young man, convicted of several murders, was sentenced to life without parole at the ripe old age of twenty-three. I asked, "How do you think God sees you?"

"Just as I'm going to rot in prison for the rest of my life," he answered, "I'll also rot in hell for eternity."

"Can God ever forgive you for these great offenses?" I asked him.

"God could never forgive me for what I've done," he answered.

I could hear the hopelessness in his voice. To him, a god who could forgive his sins was unthinkable.

But then I told him about an eleven-year-old girl named Maria Goretti who was murdered in Italy by an eighteen-year-old named Alesandro.

"What you are doing is a great sin," little Maria screamed as Alesandro tried to rape her while her mother was out of the house. He became so enraged when she told him she'd rather die than submit that he stabbed the young girl fourteen times. A family member found her and an ambulance was called to take her to the hospital. A priest came to her bedside because it was obvious she would die. As she prepared to receive Holy Communion, she totally forgave Alesandro.

He was caught, convicted, and sentenced to thirty years in prison. For many of those thirty years he lived with a frozen heart. He didn't seem to care that he had robbed Maria of her life.

Then one night he had a dream. In this dream, Maria came to him dressed in a sparkling white gown. She had flowers in her hand that gave off a brilliant glow as she held them out toward Alesandro. As he received the fourteen flowers, one for each wound he had inflicted, his heart softened. He felt Maria's forgiveness. At that moment he realized he had committed a horrible act and was destined to spend eternity in hell unless he changed. Alesandro awoke with a start and began a life of penance and prayer. The rest of his life was spent trying to atone for the life taken and the hurt caused. When he was finally released from prison, he went directly to Maria's mother and begged her forgiveness.

"If my daughter can forgive you on her death bed," she told him, "I can do no less." They later went to Mass and received the Sacrament of Communion together.

In 1950, Maria Goretti was made a saint by the Catholic Church because she chose to give her own life rather than offend God by the sin of impurity. She is a symbol of purity for the youth of this age.

God forgave Alesandro and he died a holy death.

God yearns for you to experience His awesome love, forgiveness, and holy presence too. No matter what you may have done, His mercy is infinite—immeasurably great, unbounded, unlimited, endless. Reach out to Him now. Not tomorrow. Now!

I ask you to invite the Lord Jesus Christ into your heart. He is just waiting for an invitation.

Just say:

> *Lord Jesus I invite You into my life. I ask You to forgive me my sins and to dispel the darkness that is in me. Please, Lord, send me Your Holy Spirit. Renew me, Lord. Give me Your peace.*

"When you call me,
when you go to pray to me,
I will listen to you.
When you look for me,
you will find me.
Yes, when you seek me
with all your heart,
you will find me with you,"
says the Lord,
"and I will change your lot"
(*Jeremiah* 29:12-14).

René Kieda

is a deacon in the Roman Catholic Church and the founder of Youth on Fire Ministries. He has a degree in religious and biblical studies, has worked in prison ministry for the last twelve years and in youth ministry for the last twenty years. He is presently a prison chaplain in the state of Connecticut and Coordinator of Youth Programs for the Charismatic Renewal in the Archdiocese of Hartford, CT.

"My mission is to inspire and motivate
young people to see the
great gift that God has for them,
the great treasure
that has been prepared for them
since the beginning of the world!"

Deacon Kieda is available for speaking engagements. You may contact him at:

Youth on Fire Ministries
P.O. Box 110
Enfield, CT 06083-0110

"Stir into flame the gift of God."
—2 Timothy 1:6